PCI DSS Version 4.0

A guide to the Payment Card Industry Data Security
Standard

PCI DSS Version 4.0

A guide to the Payment Card Industry Data Security Standard

STEPHEN HANCOCK

IT Governance Publishing

IT Governance Publishing Ltd
Unit 3, Clive Court
Bartholomew's Walk
Cambridgeshire Business Park
Ely, Cambridgeshire
CB7 4EA
United Kingdom
www.itgovernancepublishing.co.uk

© Stephen Hancock 2024

The author has asserted the rights of the author under the Copyright, Designs and Patents Act, 1988, to be identified as the author of this work.

Originally published in the United Kingdom in 2008 by IT Governance Publishing as _PCI DSS – A pocket guide_.

This version published in the United Kingdom in 2024 by IT Governance Publishing.

ISBN 978-1-78778-507-6

FOREWORD

All target dates for compliance with the PCI DSS have long since passed. The Standard is now on its fourth version, v3.2.1 having been withdrawn from 31 March 2024. Many organisations around the world – particularly those that fall below the top tier of payment card transaction volumes – are not yet compliant.

There are three possible reasons for this.

The first is that, outside a few US states, the PCI DSS has no legal status: it is not a law and does not have the force of law. Enforcement can only be carried out by contractual means, in a competitive payment card marketplace. The UK's Information Commissioner, however, has said that compliance with the PCI DSS shows due diligence in protecting cardholder data, and has effectively imposed it as law through the threat of fines if non-compliant at the time of a breach.[1]

The second is that enforcement is driven by the card payment brands, through the banks that have the commercial relationships with the merchants that are supposed to comply. While enforcement has become more rigorous over the past few years, it is still inconsistent.

The third is that the PCI DSS is extremely prescriptive, and takes a determined one-size-fits-all approach to information security requirements. Compliance is therefore seen as both expensive and bureaucratic. Version 4 attempts to address this through what it calls the

---

[1] _https://ico.org.uk/media/for-organisations/guide-to-the-general-data-protection-regulation-gdpr/security-1-0.pdf_.

"customized approach". However, this is likely to be suitable for only a minority of organisations.

As a result, many merchants have tried to avoid compliance. However, this is a short-sighted and high-risk stance to adopt – rather like assuming that your organisation has no exposure to acts of nature or IT failure and does not, therefore, require a business or IT service continuity plan.

All organisations that accept payment cards are prey for criminal hackers and criminal gangs seeking to steal payment card and individual identity details. Many attacks are highly automated, seeking out website and payment card system vulnerabilities remotely, using increasingly sophisticated tools and techniques. When a vulnerability is discovered, an attack can start – with the management and staff of the target organisation unaware of what is going on.

Most breaches go undetected for months, and are often found by third parties, such as payment brands conducting fraud checks. When the attack is exposed, the target organisation faces a harsh and expensive set of repercussions. These range from customer desertion and brand damage to significant penalties and operating requirements imposed by their acquiring bank, including monitoring at a level normally applicable to only the very largest of merchants. Penalties can also include expensive forensic investigation by accredited PCI Forensic Investigators (PFIs), or being made designated entities by the payment brands or the acquirers, requiring an additional level of validation to prove compliance in the future.

The PCI DSS is designed to ensure that merchants are protecting cardholder data effectively. It recognises that not all merchants have the technical understanding to identify the necessary steps and short circuits to avoid danger. All merchants and their service providers should therefore ensure that they comply with the Standard, and that they stay compliant. If the solution cannot be found internally or through the service provider, then training and consultancy is the solution.

Above all else, if every merchant cooperates in the fight against the theft of cardholder data, we might make it easier in the long run for our payment card customers.

ABOUT THE AUTHOR

Stephen Hancock is a highly experienced cyber security consultant and auditor. He has been a PCI Qualified Security Assessor for more than ten years. He has advised on the PCI DSS and conducted assessments internationally for many clients, ranging from multinational retailers to start-up fintech organisations and payment service providers. Stephen has been involved in developing and delivering training courses for the PCI DSS and ISO 27001, and holds a number of information security qualifications.

ACKNOWLEDGEMENTS

The PCI DSS, copies of which are freely available (although subject to licence) from the PCI Security Standards Council (PCI SSC), is, of course, the PCI SSC's copyright. This guide is not a substitute for acquiring and reading the Standard itself. Every reader of this guide should obtain a copy of the PCI DSS from:

www.pcisecuritystandards.org/document_library.

This guide contains many references to, and summaries of, material that is freely and more comprehensively available on the PCI SSC website and elsewhere. It is intended to be a handy, comprehensive reference tool that contains in one place all the information that anyone dealing with the PCI DSS and related issues might need. It is also a guide, not a comprehensive manual on implementing the Standard.

IT Governance offers dedicated PCI DSS courses at both foundation and implementation levels, allowing organisations to quickly get to grips with PCI DSS requirements.[2]

---

[2] *www.itgovernance.co.uk/shop/category/pci-dss-training-courses*.

CONTENTS

Chapter 1: What is the Payment Card Industry Data Security Standard (PCI DSS)? 1

Chapter 2: High-profile cardholder breaches 5

Chapter 3: What is the scope of the PCI DSS? 7

Chapter 4: Compliance and compliance programmes 9

Chapter 5: Consequences of a breach 13

Chapter 6: How do you comply with the requirements of the Standard? 15

Chapter 7: Maintaining compliance 27

Chapter 8: PCI DSS – the Standard 29

Chapter 9: Aspects of PCI DSS compliance 33

Chapter 10: The PCI self-assessment questionnaire (SAQ) 49

Chapter 11: Procedures and qualifications 55

Chapter 12: The PCI DSS and ISO/IEC 27001 59

Chapter 13: The Software Security Framework (SSF) 61

Chapter 14: PIN Transaction Security (PTS) 63

Chapter 15: Point-to-point encryption (P2PE) 65

Chapter 16: Software-based PIN entry on commercial off-the-shelf (COTS) devices 67

Further reading 69

CHAPTER 1: WHAT IS THE PAYMENT CARD INDUSTRY DATA SECURITY STANDARD (PCI DSS)?

The Payment Card Industry Data Security Standard (PCI DSS) was developed by the five founding payment brands of the PCI Security Standards Council (PCI SSC, at *www.pcisecuritystandards.org*): American Express, Discover Financial Services, JCB International, Mastercard and Visa. These were subsequently joined by UnionPay as a strategic member.

The PCI DSS consists of a standardised, industry-wide set of requirements and processes for security management, policies, procedures, network architecture, software design and critical protective measures.

The requirements of the PCI DSS must be met by all organisations (merchants and service providers) that transmit, process or store payment card data, or directly or indirectly affect the security of cardholder data. If an organisation uses a third party to manage cardholder data, it has a responsibility to ensure that the third party is compliant with the PCI DSS.

The PCI DSS (sometimes referred to as a compliance standard) is not a law. It is a contractual obligation applied and enforced – by means of fines or other restrictions – directly by the acquiring banks and card brands themselves.

The currently applicable version of the PCI DSS, since April 2024, is version 4; subject to licence, it can be freely downloaded.[3] It is published and controlled by the PCI SSC on behalf of its six founding and strategic members.

In June 2015, the PCI SSC introduced the concept of 'designated entities'. These are high-risk entities that can be prescribed a set of supplemental validation requirements to demonstrate ongoing security efforts to protect payments.

The PCI SSC also defines qualifications for Qualified Security Assessors (QSAs), Internal Security Assessors (ISAs), PCI Forensic Investigators (PFIs), PCI Professionals (PCIPs), Qualified Integrators and Resellers (QIRs) and Approved Scanning Vendors (ASVs). It trains, tests, certifies and runs quality assurance programmes for these certifications.

The PCI DSS is a set of 12 requirements that are imposed on merchants and other related parties. These requirements are described later in this guide.

Key definitions[4], acronyms and initialisms in the PCI DSS

- **Acquirer** – a bank that acquires merchants – i.e. the bank with which you have your bank account for receiving card payments.
- **Payment brand** – Visa, Mastercard, American Express, Discover, JCB, UnionPay.
- **Merchant** – sells products to cardholders.

---

[3] *www.pcisecuritystandards.org/document_library*.
[4] There is a formal English glossary available at *www.pcisecuritystandards.org/document_library*.

- **Service provider** – a business entity that is directly or indirectly involved in the processing, storage, transmission and switching of cardholder data. This includes organisations that provide services to merchants, other service providers, or members that control or could impact the security of cardholder data. Sometimes known as a third-party service provider (TPSP).

  Service providers include:
  - **Third-party processors (TPPs),** which process payment card transactions (including payment gateways); and
  - **Data storage entities (DSEs)**, which store or transmit payment card data.
- **Primary account number (PAN)** – the up-to-19-digit payment card number.
- **Qualified Security Assessor (QSA)** – someone who is trained and certified to carry out PCI DSS compliance assessments.
- **Internal Security Assessor (ISA)** – someone who is trained and certified to conduct internal security assessments.
- **Approved Scanning Vendor (ASV)** – an organisation that is approved as competent to carry out the security scans required by the PCI DSS.
- **PCI Forensic Investigator (PFI)** – a person trained and certified to investigate and contain information security breaches involving cardholder data.

CHAPTER 2: HIGH-PROFILE CARDHOLDER BREACHES

E-commerce breaches

There have been a number of high-profile attacks by the threat group Magecart, including major breaches of British Airways and Ticketmaster UK. In both incidents, a script was used to intercept cardholders' details as they entered them into a browser on the cardholders' own computers:

- In the British Airways breach, Magecart got a modified script onto the web server and application itself.
- In the case of Ticketmaster UK, Magecart got a substitute script onto a service provider's server. The malicious script was then called from the Ticketmaster website and captured card details.

In the case of British Airways, server and application access controls should have prevented the script from being modified, and change detection should have recognised that the script had been changed. Ticketmaster, meanwhile, should have ensured that the service provider was PCI DSS compliant, as the script was being called from the web page that hosted payment entry.

Hospitality industry

Criminal hackers have for several years targeted the point-of-sale (POS) equipment used to take payments in order to steal cardholder data, breaching numerous restaurant and hotel chains:

- Two million customer credit cards were stolen between May 2018 and March 2019 from more than 100 restaurants belonging to Earl Enterprises. The restaurants, which include Planet Hollywood, Buca di Beppo, and Earl of Sandwich, had their POS terminals infected with malware; the stolen credit card numbers were on sale less than a month later.

- Malware was found on payment processing servers used at restaurants and bars in the InterContinental Hotels Group in 2017. Stolen data included cardholder names, card numbers, expiration dates and internal verification codes.

- US coffee chain Caribou Coffee announced a security breach after it discovered unauthorised access to its POS systems between 28 August and 3 December 2018. 239 of its 603 shops were impacted – amounting to roughly 40% of its sites.

In these cases, and many more, isolating the cardholder data environment (CDE) from the rest of the organisation's network and implementing strong access controls would have helped protect cardholder data.

CHAPTER 3: WHAT IS THE SCOPE OF THE PCI DSS?

The PCI DSS is applicable if you store, process or transmit cardholder data, or if you are responsible for third parties that store, process or transmit cardholder data. It also applies if you are involved with or can affect the security of the storage, processing or transmission of cardholder data. The cardholder data environment (CDE) is any network or environment that processes cardholder data or sensitive authentication data. The PCI DSS does *not* apply to your organisation if primary account numbers (PANs) are not stored, processed or transmitted. The PCI DSS applies to any type of media on which card data may be held – this includes not only hard disk drives, floppy disks, magnetic tape and backup media but also printed or handwritten credit and debit card receipts where the full card number is printed. These receipts are sometimes held by merchants as a paper record of the transaction and may be used for voucher recovery purposes or as evidence of the transaction if the acquirer issues a request for information (RFI). If the card number is recorded in full, the record is in scope for the PCI DSS and must be stored securely.

Retailers must also secure all other areas where card details may be stored, processed or transmitted. Electronic point-of-sale (EPOS) systems are worthy of particular note. While newer EPOS systems store card details securely, many older ones do not. If the equipment does not store these securely, or there is uncertainty about whether it is secure, retailers should take firmer measures to protect the equipment, or upgrade to equipment that meets PCI DSS standards.

3: What is the scope of the PCI DSS?

The PCI DSS applies to all processes, people and technology, and all system components, including network components, servers or applications that are in the CDE. This includes systems that do not directly store, process or transmit cardholder data but which are connected to those that do as, if compromised, these could provide a gateway into the CDE. It includes systems that can affect the security of the cardholder data. It also applies to telephone recording technology used by call centres that accept payment card transactions. Online shopping carts and payment processing facilities are examples of applications to which the PCI DSS applies (also see Chapter 13 on the Software Security Framework (SSF)).

While not a specific requirement, the PCI DSS strongly recommends that any merchant or service provider seeks to reduce the scope of its CDE. This reduces the cost and complexity of both the initial assessment and the maintenance of PCI controls. Reducing the scope is typically achieved by reducing the number of systems and processes that are involved with cardholder data and isolating (network segmenting) the CDE. Given the complexity of modern IT networks and applications, we advise seeking the advice of a qualified PCI DSS consultant before completing this activity.

CHAPTER 4: COMPLIANCE AND COMPLIANCE PROGRAMMES

Payment brands enforce the compliance process through contractual means, including higher processing fees, fines and financial penalties for non-compliance. These penalties can be applied monthly during the remediation process, and additional fines can be levied for breaches.

What are the consequences for my business if I do not comply with the PCI DSS?

"The PCI Security Standards Council encourages all businesses that store payment account data to comply with the PCI DSS to help lower their brand and financial risks associated with account payment data compromises. The PCI Security Standards Council does not manage compliance programs and does not impose any consequences for non-compliance. Individual payment brands, however, may have their own compliance initiatives, including financial or operational consequences to certain businesses that are not compliant."[5]

There are no standardised penalties across all the payment brands, and the PCI SSC has no plans to create any. Because individual payment brands have their own

---

[5] *https://www.pcisecuritystandards.org/faq/articles/Frequently_Asked_Question/What-are-the-consequences-to-my-business-if-I-do-not-comply-with-the-PCI-DSS/*. Article number 1015: "What are the consequences to my business if I do not comply with the PCI DSS?"

compliance initiatives, each requires separate evidence of compliance. Since Visa and Mastercard do not have a direct contractual relationship with individual merchants, they enforce the PCI DSS through the merchants' acquiring banks. This means that each acquiring bank will take whatever action it thinks it can make stick, commercially, to enforce the PCI DSS. The acquiring bank is usually the best channel through which to discuss compliance deadlines and penalties, which are all imposed by means of the payment brand/acquiring bank's contract with the merchant.

While the PCI DSS is a common standard, each payment brand has its own compliance programme. Note that there are regional variations for Visa (e.g. USA and Europe), while Mastercard has a single global standard, and that acquiring banks – not the payment brands – are usually responsible for enforcement. All detailed compliance enquiries should therefore be directed to your acquiring bank. Detailed on the next page are the websites for the PCI DSS compliance programmes for each of the five founding members of the PCI SSC, which will give some guidance on the compliance actions that might be expected in respect of each of the payment brands.

Many merchants use a third-party payment service provider as an intermediary between themselves and their acquiring bank. (Some organisations act as both payment service provider and acquiring bank.) Since the payment brands and acquiring banks do not have a direct contractual relationship with the payment service provider, they cannot use this to enforce compliance. However, they maintain lists of compliant service providers and can contractually require their merchants to use only listed service providers. Merchants should also ensure through contracts that any service providers they use for services such as data centre hosting or website hosting are compliant.

Contact details for the payment brands are kept on the PCI SSC website and regularly updated as part of the FAQ section.[6]

American Express

Website: *http://www.americanexpress.com/datasecurity*
Email: *AmericanExpressCompliance@securetrust.com*

Discover

Website: *https://www.discovernetwork.com/en-us/*
For questions about the Discover Information Security & Compliance (DISC) programme:
https://www.discovernetwork.com/en-us/business-resources/fraud-security/pci-rules-regulations/

Email: *DISCCompliance@discover.com*

JCB

Website: *http://www.global.jcb/en/products/security/data-security-program/*
Email: *riskmanagement@info.jcb.co.jp*

Mastercard

Website: *http://www.mastercard.com/sdp*
Email: *sdp@mastercard.com*

UnionPay

Website: *http://unionpayintl.com/en/*
Email: *risk@unionpayintl.com*

---

[6]*https://www.pcisecuritystandards.org/faq/articles/Frequently_Asked_Question/How-do-I-contact-the-payment-card-brands/*. Article number 1142: "How do I contact the payment card brands?"

Visa – Canada, US

Website: *http://www.visa.com/cisp*
Email: *cisp@visa.com*

Visa – Latin America and the Caribbean

Website: *http://www.visa.com/cisp*
Email: *aislac@visa.com*

Visa Europe

Website: *http://www.visaeurope.com/ais*
Email: *datasecuritystandards@visa.com* (for member and merchant requirements)
Email: *pcidsseurope@visa.com* (for service provider requirements)

Visa – Central Europe, Middle East and Africa

Website: *http://www.visa.com/cisp*
Email: *pcicemea@visa.com*

CHAPTER 5: CONSEQUENCES OF A BREACH

The consequences of a data security breach are likely to be proportionate to the seriousness of the breach and the extent to which the merchant or service provider is able to demonstrate prior compliance with the PCI DSS. The penalties can be any or all of the following:

- A significant cost for a forensic investigation.
- The merchant automatically becoming a level 1 merchant (i.e. yearly on-site audits).
- A possible charge by issuer(s) to acquirer(s) for card reissue, which may be passed on to the merchant.
- The merchant may lose its ability to accept payment cards.
- Transaction costs may be increased.
- Service providers may be removed from listings by the payment brands.
- Merchants or service providers may become designated entities and subject to additional validation requirements.
- Possible regulator fines (because cardholder data is personal information).

For level 1 merchants, the combination of fines, litigation and brand damage is significant; for non-level-1 merchants, the consequences of a breach can be just as serious.

CHAPTER 6: HOW DO YOU COMPLY WITH THE REQUIREMENTS OF THE STANDARD?

For all organisations that must comply with the PCI DSS, there are two options for demonstrating compliance: an annual on-site security audit by a QSA or an ISA and the submission of four passing quarterly network scans by an ASV (where applicable), or completion of a self-assessment questionnaire (SAQ) and the submission of four passing quarterly ASV network scans. Which option applies is determined by an organisation's transaction volume and whether it has previously suffered a security breach.

The major global payment brands require that every entity – including financial institutions, merchants and service providers – that stores, processes or transmits payment card data, in every channel – including catalogue and online retailers, as well as bricks-and-mortar businesses – must comply with the PCI DSS.

Merchant PCI DSS compliance criteria

Compliance requirements are dependent on a merchant's activity level. Visa and Mastercard define four broadly comparable levels, based on the annual number of credit/debit card transactions. (The other card brands may define levels a little differently.) While payment brands determine the compliance levels for their own brands, acquirers are usually responsible for determining the compliance validation requirement levels of their merchants. The compliance levels are based on the following table and usually refer to the number of transactions of each payment brand in a year. Whether transaction volume applies only to e-commerce transactions or to payments processed through all channels is decided separately by each payment brand, but, in general, all transactions are included.

Table 1: Merchant PCI DSS Compliance Levels

Level 1 criteria:

American Express

2.5 million American Express card transactions or more per year.

Any merchant that has had a data incident.

Any merchant that American Express otherwise deems a level 1.

Visa

Merchants processing more than 6 million Visa transactions per year via all channels.

Global merchants identified as level 1 by any Visa region.

Mastercard

Any merchant having more than 6 million total combined Mastercard and Maestro transactions per year.

Any merchant that has suffered a hack or an attack that resulted in an account data compromise.

Any merchant meeting Visa's level 1 criteria.

Any merchant that Mastercard determines should meet the level 1 merchant requirements to minimise risk to the system.

Discover

All merchants processing more than 6 million card transactions per year on the Discover network.

Any merchant that Discover determines should meet the level 1 compliance validation and reporting requirements.

All merchants required by another payment brand or acquirer to validate and report their compliance as a level 1 merchant.

JCB

1 million JCB transactions or more per year for merchants (excluding Internet payment service providers (IPSPs)).

All IPSPs regardless of volume.

Level 1 validation requirements:

Annual on-site audit by a QSA or an ISA, passing ASV scans and submitting a Report on Compliance (RoC).

Level 2 criteria:

American Express

50,000 to 2.5 million American Express card transactions per year.

Visa/Mastercard/Discover

Merchants processing 1 to 6 million transactions per year, across all the brand's channels.

JCB

Fewer than 1 million JCB transactions per year for merchants (excluding IPSPs).

Level 2 validation requirements:

Annual SAQ, passing a quarterly scan by an ASV.

In addition to passing quarterly network scans by an ASV, Mastercard requires an on-site assessment by a QSA if any of SAQ A, SAQ A-E or SAQ D apply, which, in practice, will be almost all level 2 merchants.

Quarterly network scans by an ASV are only a requirement on some SAQ forms; check the requirements with the payment brand compliance programmes.

Level 3 criteria:

American Express (designated)

10,000 to 50,000 American Express card transactions per year and has been designated by American Express as being required to submit validation documents. American Express will contact these designated merchants and provide them with details for reporting their security status by submitting PCI validation documents.

American Express

Fewer than 50,000 American Express card transactions per year (recommended to submit an SAQ and ASV scans).

Visa

Merchants processing 20,000 to 1 million Visa e-commerce transactions per year, across all the brand's channels.

Mastercard

Merchants processing 20,000 to 1 million Mastercard and Maestro e-commerce transactions per year.

Any merchant meeting Visa's level 3 criteria.

Discover

All other merchants.

Level 3 validation requirements:

Quarterly scan by an ASV.

Annual SAQ.

Level 4 criteria:

American Express

Fewer than 10,000 American Express transactions per year.

Visa

E-commerce merchants processing fewer than 20,000 Visa e-commerce transactions annually.

Non-e-commerce merchants processing up to 1 million Visa transactions annually.

Mastercard

All other merchants.

Level 4 validation requirements:

Annual SAQ.

Quarterly scan by an ASV (may be recommended or required, depending on acquirer compliance criteria).

Special designations:

American Express (EMV)

50,000 or more American Express chip-enabled card transactions per year with at least 75% made on an EMV-enabled (chip-enabled) terminal capable of processing contact and contactless American Express transactions.

American Express (EMV) validation requirements

Annual EMV Attestation (AEA) (required).

The PCI SSC is clear that PCI DSS compliance is required even if there is only one payment card transaction per year. However, it is down to the card brands and acquiring banks to enforce this.

Service provider PCI DSS compliance criteria

A service provider is an organisation involved in the processing, storage and transmission of cardholder data, and/or protecting the security of cardholder data, but which is not a merchant or a card brand member. Hosting providers and others providing services to merchants would also fall into this category.

Service provider compliance requirements are defined by the payment brands. Visa, Mastercard and American Express categorise service providers according to transaction volume and/or type of service provider. In comparison with the four levels of merchant compliance criteria, there are only two for service providers.

Table 2: Service Provider PCI DSS Compliance Levels

Level 1 criteria:

American Express

2.5 million American Express card transactions or more per year, or any other service provider that American Express otherwise deems a level 1 service provider.

Visa

VisaNet processors or any service provider that stores, processes and/or transmits more than 300,000 Visa transactions annually.

Mastercard

All Third-Party Processors (TPPs).

All Staged Digital Wallet Operators (SDWOs).

All Digital Activity Service Providers (DASPs).

All Token Service Providers (TSPs).

All 3-D Secure Service Providers (3-DSSPs).

All Instalment Service Providers (ISPs).

All Merchant Payment Gateways (MPGs).

All Data Storage Entities (DSEs) and Payment Facilitators (PFs) with more than 300,000 total combined Mastercard and Maestro transactions annually.

Discover

All service providers that store, process and/or transmit more than 300,000 Discover card transactions per year.

Any service provider that Discover, at its sole discretion, determines should meet the level 1 compliance validation and reporting requirements.

JCB

All TPPs with 1 million or more transactions.

Level 1 validation requirements:

Visa, Mastercard and American Express

Annual on-site review by a QSA.

Quarterly network scan by an ASV.

Level 2 criteria:

American Express

Fewer than 2.5 million transactions.

Visa

Any service provider that stores, processes and/or transmits fewer than 300,000 Visa transactions annually.

Mastercard

All DSEs and PFs with 300,000 or fewer total combined Mastercard and Maestro transactions annually.

All Terminal Servicers (TSs).

Discover

All service providers that store, process and/or transmit fewer than 300,000 Discover card transactions per year.

> **JCB**
>
> All TPPs with fewer than 1 million transactions.
>
> **Level 2 validation requirements:**
>
> *Visa, Mastercard and American Express*
>
> Annual SAQ. Quarterly network scan by an ASV.

Designated entities will have to complete an additional set of requirements within an appendix to the main PCI DSS. An acquirer or a payment brand will determine if an organisation requires additional validation. As designated entities, it is very likely they will also be made a level 1 merchant or service provider.

Role of service providers

Many service providers deliver payment services directly to merchants using a variety of online and physical technologies. These services include online payment gateways, traditional document processing facilities and shared hosting server and application providers. The PCI DSS asks that shared hosting providers ensure compliance with additional requirements, which include protecting each merchant's hosted individual CDE, ensuring the availability of audit trails and allowing forensic investigation if required. To achieve compliance, a merchant must ensure that any service provider it uses is PCI DSS compliant.

Service providers that have an indirect connection with the storage, processing or transmission of cardholder data – such as an IT support company that manages the firewalls in the perimeter of the CDE and hence can affect the inbound and outbound traffic – are also required to be PCI DSS compliant.

Service providers demonstrate their compliance with the PCI DSS by validation, as outlined in Table 2. The PCI DSS requires that, in addition to achieving compliance with the requirements of the Standard, service providers should also provide supporting evidence (e.g. via an Attestation of Compliance (AoC)) to prove to merchants that they are compliant. Service providers and merchants must agree in writing which aspects of the PCI DSS requirements the service provider is responsible for ensuring compliance with and which the merchant is responsible for. Merchants must maintain a list of service providers and the compliant services they provide.

Service providers can register their compliance with the card brands and be listed on their websites.

Online payment gateways

We strongly recommend that merchants that sell their products or services online use a third-party payment gateway service that is fully PCI compliant. These services are available from PayPal, Opayo, Stripe, Worldpay, Global Payments, Barclays ePDQ, and others. For smaller e-commerce businesses, outsourcing to a payment gateway service is a cost-effective way of ensuring PCI compliance.

Please note that such a merchant (likely to be level 3 or 4) will be required to complete the relevant SAQ and submit the results of a quarterly scan by an ASV. The SAQ document required will be SAQ A for those that have a fully outsourced e-commerce platform, SAQ A-EP for those that use only partially outsourced e-commerce platforms, or SAQ C-VT, which applies to merchants that use web-based virtual terminals to manually enter payment card information. See Chapter 10, Table 3 for further information.

A number of these service providers provide tools and support for merchants to complete and submit PCI DSS compliance documentation. In some cases, the service provider, especially if it is also the merchant acquiring bank, will automate the process and complete the documentation for the merchant providing the merchant has implemented the solution in exactly the way the service provider has stated.

CHAPTER 7: MAINTAINING COMPLIANCE

Once an organisation has achieved compliance with the PCI DSS, it must maintain its level of compliance. This means being aware of any changes to the PCI DSS itself (the latest version was released in March 2022 and took effect from 1 April 2024), as well as maintaining the PCI DSS security environment.

Any changes to in-scope systems, processes and technologies must be implemented in a PCI DSS-compliant manner, and their effect on compliance assessed and recorded. If it is a significant change, all requirements that are mandatory to be revaluated after a significant change must be completed and the result recorded.

All applicable PCI DSS processes must be followed and maintained at all times throughout the period between recertifications. While assessment and attestation are annual events, compliance is continuous and should be part of business as usual.

The PCI SSC makes the point this way: technically, it is true that if you have completed an SAQ, you are compliant – *"for that particular moment in time when the Self-Assessment Questionnaire and associated vulnerability scan (if applicable) is completed. After that moment, only a post-breach forensic analysis can prove PCI compliance. But a bad system change can make you non-compliant in an instant. True security of cardholder data requires non-*

stop assessment and remediation to ensure that likelihood of a breach is kept as low as possible. "[7]

Version 3.2 of the PCI DSS incorporated the requirements for designated entities supplemental validation (DESV) as an appendix to the Standard called Appendix A3. Although the DESV/Appendix A3 is only mandated for those entities that have been designated, the PCI SSC recommends that the controls be used to complement any entity's PCI DSS compliance efforts, and all entities are encouraged to follow them as a best practice, even if they are not required to validate.

Version 4 of the PCI DSS contains some new requirements that are not mandated until after 31 March 2025. Until then, these requirements may be marked 'Not applicable'.

---

[7] *www.pcisecuritystandards.org/documents/pciscc_ten_common_myths. pdf* (Myth 8).

CHAPTER 8: PCI DSS – THE STANDARD

The PCI DSS has 12 principal requirements, organised into 6 control objectives. Note that this guide is no substitute for obtaining your own copy of the Standard, which is freely downloadable:
www.pcisecuritystandards.org/security_standards/docum ents.php.

PCI DSS version 1.0 was originally published in January 2005, and subsequently updated to version 1.1 in September 2006 and version 1.2 in October 2008. PCI DSS version 2.0 was released on 28 October 2010. Version 3.0 was published on 7 November 2013, with version 3.1 released in April 2015, version 3.2 in April 2016 and version 3.2.1 in May 2018. The current iteration, version 4, was released in March 2022.

With the release of PCI DSS version 2.0, the PCI SSC introduced a three-year lifecycle for standards development. This ensured a gradual and phased introduction of new versions, and helps prevent organisations from becoming non-compliant when a new version is published.

Version 3.0 of the PCI DSS introduced more flexibility in implementing the Standard's requirements, and increased the focus on education, awareness and security as a shared responsibility.

Version 3.1 was an out-of-band update created in response to the repeated vulnerabilities discovered in the SSL security protocol in early 2015. It removes SSL and early versions of TLS as secure technologies, and dictates that they are replaced with TLSv1.2 and beyond, or IPsec.

Since version 3.1, however, the PCI SSC has abandoned the three-year cycle in favour of more frequent incremental updates to help the Standard keep up with a faster pace of change within the security industry.

Version 3.2 was an incremental update introducing business-as-usual (BAU) requirements. Organisations have typically focused on the annual assessment rather than continually managing their compliance state. Compliance is often only at its peak following the annual assessment, and trails off over time. Version 3.2 targets service providers by adding guidance for maintaining card security as part of their BAU activities.

Appendix A3 was added to state the requirements for designated entities, and Appendix A2 was added to provide clear guidance on transitioning from using SSL and early TLS, with extended timescales provided for transitions supported by formal risk assessments and mitigation plans.

Version 4

The 6 control objectives and 12 PCI DSS requirements that address these are as follows:

Build and maintain a secure network and systems

- **"Requirement 1**: *Install and maintain network security controls. "*

- **"Requirement 2**: *Apply secure configurations to all system components. "*

Protect account data

- **"Requirement 3**: *Protect stored account data. "*

- **"Requirement 4**: *Protect cardholder data with strong cryptography during transmission over open, public networks. "*

Maintain a vulnerability management programme

- **"Requirement 5**: *Protect all systems and networks from malicious software."*

- **"Requirement 6**: *Develop and maintain secure systems and software."*

Implement strong access control measures

- **"Requirement 7**: *Restrict access to system components and cardholder data by business need-to-know."*

- **"Requirement 8**: *Identify users and authenticate access to system components."*

- **"Requirement 9**: *Restrict physical access to cardholder data."*

Regularly monitor and test networks

- **"Requirement 10**: *Log and monitor all access to system components and cardholder data."*

- **"Requirement 11**: *Test security of systems and networks regularly."*

Maintain an information security policy

- **"Requirement 12**: *Support information security with organizational policies and programs."*[8]

---

[8] PCI DSS v4.0. For more information, visit: *https://www.pcisecuritystandards.org/*.

CHAPTER 9: ASPECTS OF PCI DSS COMPLIANCE

Requirement 1 (Install and maintain network security controls)

Requirement 1 is concerned with controlling network traffic into and out of the cardholder data environment (CDE). This includes traffic to and from the Internet and between internal trusted and untrusted networks ('untrusted' meaning a network not assessed for PCI compliance).

Older versions of the PCI DSS referred to firewalls and routers, but version 4 refers to network security controls (NSCs), recognising the technologies such as security groups used in Cloud environments.

The sub-requirements are as follows:

- Processes and mechanisms for installing and maintaining network security controls are defined and understood.
- Network security controls (NSCs) are configured and maintained.
- Network access to and from the cardholder data environment is restricted.
- Network connections between trusted and untrusted networks are controlled.
- Risks to the CDE from computing devices that are able to connect to both untrusted networks and the CDE are mitigated.

Points to be aware of:

- In common with all requirements through to requirement 11, requirement 1 now starts by requiring documented security policies and procedures and documented roles and responsibilities.
- Rulesets controlling the inbound and outbound traffic need to be documented along with the business justification for the rules.

Requirement 2 (Apply secure configurations to all system components)

Data breaches often occur as a result of vulnerabilities introduced by errors in system and configurations. Requirement 2 is concerned with ensuring that all components, including servers and network devices, are securely configured in line with best practice.

The sub-requirements are as follows:

- Processes and mechanisms for applying secure configurations to all system components are defined and understood.
- System components are configured and managed securely.
- Wireless environments are configured and managed securely.

Points to be aware of:

- System configuration standards for each type of component in scope need to be documented and available for the assessor to review. These should be consistent with industry-accepted system hardening standards or vendor hardening recommendations.

Requirement 3 (Protect stored account data)

Requirement 3 is at the heart of the PCI DSS since it is concerned with protecting stored account data. It includes requirements for limiting storage, not storing sensitive authentication data (SAD), and encryption and key management.

The sub-requirements are as follows:

- Processes and mechanisms for protecting stored account data are defined and understood.
- Storage of account data is kept to a minimum.
- Sensitive authentication data (SAD) is not stored after authorisation.
- Access to displays of full PAN and the ability to copy cardholder data are restricted.
- PAN is secured wherever it is stored.
- Cryptographic keys used to protect stored account data are secured.
- Where cryptography is used to protect stored account data, key-management processes and procedures covering all aspects of the key lifecycle are defined and implemented.

Points to be aware of:

- The best way to simplify PCI DSS compliance is to avoid storing cardholder data. Where the PAN is replaced with an irreversible token or the PAN is sufficiently truncated, these are considered not in scope.
- As with earlier versions of the PCI DSS, PANs may be stored using hashing, but in version 4 the hashes

must now use cryptographic keys with all the associated key management.

- Service providers must have a documented description of the cryptographic architecture.

Requirement 4 (Protect cardholder data with strong cryptography during transmission over open, public networks)

Requirement 4 is focused on protecting cardholder data when it is transmitted over public networks. For example, transmission over the Internet from an e-commerce customer to a merchant or from a merchant to a payment service provider.

The sub-requirements are as follows:

- Processes and mechanisms for protecting cardholder data with strong cryptography during transmission over open, public networks are defined and documented.
- PAN is protected with strong cryptography during transmission.

Points to be aware of:

- Open public networks also include Wi-Fi, Bluetooth, and cellular and satellite communications.
- Version 4 has new requirements, effective after 31 March 2025, for validating SSL certificates and maintaining an inventory of keys and certificates.

Requirement 5 (Protect all systems and networks from malicious software)

Malware remains a ubiquitous threat to computer systems, and attackers continue to use it successfully as ransomware or to exfiltrate data. Requirement 5 is aimed at managing this threat through technical controls.

The sub-requirements are as follows:

- Processes and mechanisms for protecting all systems and networks from malicious software are defined and understood.
- Malicious software (malware) is prevented, or detected and addressed.
- Anti-malware mechanisms and processes are active, maintained and monitored.
- Anti-phishing mechanisms protect users against phishing attacks.

Points to be aware of:

- Version 4 allows the use of next-generation anti-malware that uses behavioural analysis instead of scanning. Previously, scanning was mandated.
- The anti-malware solution must generate logs, which are retained for 12 months with 3 months immediately available.
- Because phishing is such a common method of introducing malware and launching other attacks, there is a new requirement that entities must deploy automated mechanisms to protect against phishing.

Requirement 6 (Develop and maintain secure systems and software)

Attackers often exploit vulnerabilities in commercial, open-source and bespoke software. Requirement 6 is concerned with protecting software through patching, secure coding and change control.

The sub-requirements are as follows:

- Processes and mechanisms for developing and maintaining secure systems and software are defined and understood.
- Bespoke and custom software are developed securely.
- Security vulnerabilities are identified and addressed.
- Public-facing web applications are protected against attacks.
- Changes to all system components are managed securely.

Points to be aware of:

- The requirements for training developers have been made more specific. Entities need to maintain records of training.
- Entities must use external sources of information about vulnerabilities (not just scanning) and must apply a risk ranking to vulnerabilities.
- Entities need an inventory of software, including third-party components included in bespoke software.
- Entities need to document their software development procedures, including change control, coding and testing, so these can be reviewed by the assessor.
- After 31 March 2025, entities must validate scripts loaded into the user's browser for payment pages.

- After 31 March 2025, public-facing web applications must be protected by an automated solution (e.g. web application firewall), not just by periodic scanning.

Requirement 7 (Restrict access to system components and cardholder data by business need-to-know)

Access control is fundamental to security. Requirement seven focuses on entities having an access control model based on what is needed for users' functions and roles and least privilege.

The sub-requirements are as follows:

- Processes and mechanisms for restricting access to system components and cardholder data by business need to know are defined and understood.
- Access to system components and data is appropriately defined and assigned.
- Access to system components and data is managed via an access control system(s).

Points to be aware of:

- Since access is required to be according to users' functions, it follows that entities must have defined and documented the roles and the necessary access required.
- There is a new requirement to review user accounts every six months.
- There is a new requirement to manage the access granted to application and system accounts.

Requirement 8 (Identify users and authenticate access to system components)

Like requirement seven, requirement eight is also about access control, but it is concerned with the technical controls including passwords and multifactor authentication (MFA).

The sub-requirements are as follows:

- Processes and mechanisms for identifying users and authenticating access to system components are defined and understood.
- User identification and related accounts for users and administrators are strictly managed throughout an account's lifecycle.
- Strong authentication for users and administrators is established and managed.
- MFA is implemented to secure access into the CDE.
- MFA systems are configured to prevent misuse.
- Use of application and system accounts and associated authentication factors is strictly managed.

Points to be aware of:

- The minimum length for passwords is increased to 12 characters (or 8 if the system will not support 12).
- The Standard allows for analysis of an account's security posture as an alternative to 90-day password changes.
- MFA is now required for all access into the CDE, not just for privileged access (but note that this requirement is not included in most of the SAQs).

- MFA may be required at two points: for remote access to a network with access to the CDE and for access to the CDE itself.

- There are new requirements relating to managing application and system accounts and passwords.

Requirement 9 (Restrict physical access to cardholder data)

Requirement nine deals with physical security. First, physical security of sensitive areas containing cardholder data, which could be data centres and might include server rooms in retail premises, contact centres and other locations. Second, controls over physical media containing cardholder data, both electronic media and hard copy. It also addresses physical security of point-of-interaction (POI) devices to prevent tampering.

The sub-requirements are as follows:

- Processes and mechanisms for restricting physical access to cardholder data are defined and understood.

- Physical access controls manage entry into facilities and systems containing cardholder data.

- Physical access for personnel and visitors is authorised and managed.

- Media with cardholder data is securely stored, accessed, distributed and destroyed.

- POI devices are protected from tampering and unauthorised substitution.

Points to be aware of:

- Entities that use Cloud hosting or colocation facilities may be able to pass responsibility for physical access control to the third party.
- Distinguishing between staff and visitors means that visitors should not be able to pass as staff simply by removing their visitor badge.
- Staff using POI devices should have specific training in relation to POI device security, not just generic information security training.

Requirement 10 (Log and monitor all access to system components and cardholder data)

Logging is part of defence in depth. Requirement ten contains controls to help identify and respond to both attempted and successful compromises. The requirements for logging are wide and cover almost any action that might take place affecting the CDE.

The sub-requirements are as follows:

- Processes and mechanisms for logging and monitoring all access to system components and cardholder data are defined and documented.
- Audit logs are implemented to support the detection of anomalies and suspicious activity, and the forensic analysis of events.
- Audit logs are protected from destruction and unauthorised modifications.
- Audit logs are reviewed to identify anomalies or suspicious activity.
- Audit log history is retained and available for analysis.
- Time-synchronisation mechanisms support consistent time settings across all systems.

- Failures of critical security control systems are detected, reported and responded to promptly.

Points to be aware of:

- The entity needs to be able to demonstrate to the assessor that the identified activities are captured in the logs for all in-scope components.
- Cloud-based solutions can meet the requirement for backing up logs to secure log servers.
- Reviewing and analysing log files is difficult and time consuming but must be done daily. After 31 March 2025, entities must use automated mechanisms to review logs. For most entities, this means using third-party tools or Cloud services.
- After 31 March 2025, all entities must monitor for the failure of security control systems. Before then, the requirement applies to service providers.

Requirement 11 (Test security of systems and networks regularly)

Testing enables an entity to identify and remediate vulnerabilities before an attacker exploits them. Requirement 11 covers vulnerability scanning and penetration testing as well as protecting web pages.

The sub-requirements are as follows:

- Processes and mechanisms for regularly testing security of systems and networks are defined and understood.
- Wireless access points are identified and monitored, and unauthorised wireless access points are addressed.

- External and internal vulnerabilities are regularly identified, prioritised and addressed.
- External and internal penetration testing is regularly performed, and exploitable vulnerabilities and security weaknesses are corrected.
- Network intrusions and unexpected file changes are detected and responded to.
- Unauthorised changes on payment pages are detected and responded to.

Points to be aware of:

- Testing for wireless is required even where wireless is not used in the CDE because the intention is to find unauthorised wireless.
- Entities should be aware of the difference between vulnerability scanning, which is passive, and penetration testing, which actively seeks to identify how vulnerabilities may be exploited.
- After 31 March 2025, entities must address not only high and critical vulnerabilities but also those ranked below high.
- Entities must write their own requirement for penetration testing, not just rely on the penetration testing supplier's methodology.
- After 31 March 2025, entities must deploy a change- and tamper-detection mechanism on payment web pages.

Requirement 12 (Support information security with organizational policies and programs)

Requirement 12 covers a range of organisational matters including policy, training, supplier relationships and personnel.

The sub-requirements are as follows:

- A comprehensive information security policy that governs and provides direction for protection of the entity's information assets is known and current.
- Acceptable use policies for end-user technologies are defined and implemented.
- Risks to the cardholder data environment are formally identified, evaluated and managed.
- PCI DSS compliance is managed.
- PCI DSS scope is documented and validated.
- Security awareness education is an ongoing activity.
- Personnel are screened to reduce risks from insider threats.
- Risk to information assets associated with third-party service provider (TPSP) relationships is managed.
- TPSPs support their customers' PCI DSS compliance.
- Suspected and confirmed security incidents that could impact the CDE are responded to immediately.

Points to be aware of:

- Requirement 12 includes the outline of the targeted risk analyses that are required to determine the frequency with which certain controls must be undertaken (5.2.3.1, 5.3.2.1, 7.2.5.1, 8.6.3, 9.5.1.2.1, 10.4.2.1, 11.3.1.1, 11.6.1).

- Entities must conduct an annual review of cryptographic suites and protocols.
- Entities must conduct an annual review of all technologies used in the CDE.
- Entities must document and confirm the scope of the CDE every 12 months. This, combined with separate requirements to maintain network diagrams (1.2.3) and card data flow diagrams (1.2.4), may require significant initial work.
- Security awareness training must include social engineering and phishing.

Compensating controls and the customized approach

When an organisation is unable to meet the strict requirements of the PCI DSS owing to legitimate and documented business or technical constraints, it is permissible to submit alternative measures. These measures are known as compensating controls, and must fully mitigate the risks associated with the requirements and meet the criteria as defined in PCI DSS Appendix B: Compensating Controls. On an annual basis, any compensating controls must be documented, reviewed and validated by the assessor and included with the RoC submission.

Whereas up to v3.2.1, the PCI DSS was highly prescriptive, version 4 introduced a more flexible concept known as the *"customized approach"*. Each requirement now has a *"Customized Approach Objective"*. The customized approach allows an entity to take an approach to meeting a requirement's Customized Approach Objective in a way that does not strictly follow the defined requirement but meets the objective in a manner unique to that organisation.

To use the customized approach, the entity must complete a risk assessment and must fully document how the control operates, how it meets the objective, how it is maintained and how it was tested. The assessor, in turn, must review this documentation and devise, document and carry out testing procedures for the control. The customized approach can only be used with an RoC; it cannot be used with an SAQ. It is intended for organisations with a well-established information security function and a mature approach to compliance.

Not applicable and not tested

It is also possible for an organisation to mark requirements as 'not applicable' if sufficient justification for the non-applicability can be provided. Further details on this are provided in the reporting instructions within the RoC and SAQ. Since all the SAQs (except SAQ D) contain a sub-set of the full set of requirements, it is understood that (provided the criteria for using the SAQ are met) all other requirements are not applicable.

It is also possible to mark requirements as 'not tested'. In this case, no consideration is given to the requirement. The entity may still be assessed as compliant, but the assessment is reported as a 'partial' assessment. Possible scenarios for this might be a merchant that wants just one payment channel out of several assessed, or a hosting service provider that wants just its physical colocation service assessed.

CHAPTER 10: THE PCI SELF-ASSESSMENT QUESTIONNAIRE (SAQ)

The PCI DSS SAQ is a validation tool developed by the PCI SSC to assist merchants and service providers in self-evaluating their compliance with the PCI DSS. Levels three and four merchants and level two service providers are usually able to report compliance using an SAQ. Level two merchants may be able to report using an SAQ but their acquiring bank may still require that an assessment is carried out and certified on the Attestation of Compliance (AoC) by a QSA. Level one merchants and service providers always require an independent assessment reported with a Report on Compliance (RoC) and an AoC.

Each SAQ is designed to address the particular subset of PCI DSS requirements that are applicable to the use of a specific payment channel. All merchants and their service providers are required to comply with the PCI DSS in its entirety and, if they are eligible for self-assessment, to attest that they comply by using the AoC document. New SAQs and AoCs were released in 2022 to meet the requirements of version 4 of the PCI DSS.

When initially released for version 4, there were nine validation categories. A tenth SAQ, software-based PIN entry on COTS (SPoC), was released in September 2023 (*see Table 3*). The SAQs can be downloaded from: *www.pcisecuritystandards.org/document_library*.

Table 3: Self-assessment Questionnaire Validation Categories

SAQ validation type	Description
A	Card-not-present (e-commerce or mail/telephone order) merchants that do not store, process or transmit any account data in electronic format on their systems or premises. All processing of account data is entirely outsourced to a PCI DSS-compliant third-party service provider (TPSP)/payment processor. For e-commerce channels, all elements of the payment page(s)/form(s) delivered to the customer's browser originate only and directly from a PCI DSS-compliant TPSP/payment processor. This never applies to face-to-face merchants.
A-EP	E-commerce merchants whose website does not receive account data but controls how customers, or their account data, are redirected to a PCI DSS-compliant TPSP/payment processor. All processing of account data, with the exception of the payment page, is entirely outsourced to a PCI DSS-compliant TPSP/payment processor and each element of the payment page(s) delivered to the customer's browser originates from either the

SAQ validation type	Description
	merchant's website or a PCI DSS-compliant TPSP. No electronic storage, processing or transmission of cardholder data. Only applies to e-commerce channels.
B	Imprint only or standalone, dial-out (via a phone line) terminal merchants. No transmission of cardholder data over data networks. No electronic storage of cardholder data. Not applicable to e-commerce channels.
B-IP	Merchants with standalone IP-connected, PIN Transaction Security (PTS)-approved terminals. The only transmission is from the terminal to the payment processor (isolated connection). No electronic storage of cardholder data. Not applicable to e-commerce channels.
C	Merchants with payment applications connected to the Internet but isolated from the rest of the environment. The physical location of the POS is not connected to other locations (single LAN only). No electronic storage of cardholder data. Not applicable to e-commerce channels.
C-VT	Merchants with web-based virtual payment terminals where the

SAQ validation type	Description
	merchant manually enters account data via a securely connected web browser. The virtual terminal system is isolated from the rest of the environment. No attached card readers and no electronic storage of cardholder data. Not applicable to e-commerce channels.
D (Merchants)	All other SAQ-eligible merchants that do not meet the criteria for any other SAQ.
D (Service Providers)	All SAQ-eligible service providers.
P2PE	Merchants using a validated PCI-listed P2PE solution. May be either bricks-and-mortar (card-present) or mail/telephone-order (card-not-present) merchants. No electronic cardholder data storage. No electronic processing or transmission of cardholder data outside of the P2PE solution. Not applicable to e-commerce channels.
SPoC	Merchants using a commercial off-the-shelf (COTS) mobile device (for example, phone or tablet) with a secure card reader that is part of a SPoC solution included on the PCI SSC's list of validated software-based PIN entry COTS (SPoC)

SAQ validation type	Description
	solutions. Not applicable to e-commerce channels.

CHAPTER 11: PROCEDURES AND QUALIFICATIONS

The PCI SSC mandates the procedures that must be followed in conducting audits and in carrying out scanning procedures. It also lays down specific requirements for qualification as a QSA or an ASV.

Qualification Requirements for Qualified Security Assessors (QSAs) v4.1

https://listings.pcisecuritystandards.org/search_result/doc uments/qsa_qual_req_v2_0

To be recognised as a QSA by the PCI SSC, QSAs must meet or exceed the requirements described in the above document and must also execute the QSA Agreement in Appendix A with the PCI SSC. Clients can provide feedback on the effectiveness of the QSA.

QSA Feedback Form

https://www.pcisecuritystandards.org/assessors_and_solu tions/qualified_security_assessors_feedback

QSA feedback is completed online.

PCI DSS Qualified Security Assessors

https://www.pcisecuritystandards.org/assessors_and_solu tions/qualified_security_assessors

This list, which is updated regularly, contains contact details for all QSAs, together with information about the markets they serve. Alternatively, you can look up individual assessors in the PCI SSC's database.

Qualification Requirements for Approved Scanning Vendors (ASVs) v3.0

https://listings.pcisecuritystandards.org/search_result/doc uments/asv_qual_req_21

Recognition as an ASV by the PCI SSC requires the ASV, its employees and its scanning solution to meet or exceed the requirements previously described and to execute the 'PCI ASV Compliance Test Agreement' set out below with the PCI SSC. The organisations that qualify are then identified on the PCI SSC's ASV list on its website.

Approved Scanning Vendors feedback

https://www.pcisecuritystandards.org/assessors_and_solu tions/approved_scanning_vendors_feedback

PCI DSS Approved Scanning Vendors

https://www.pcisecuritystandards.org/assessors_and_solu tions/approved_scanning_vendors

This list, which is updated on a regular basis, contains contact details for all approved ASVs. Any ASV that carries out a scan must be on the list when the scan is carried out.

ASV Program Guide 4.0

https://www.pcisecuritystandards.org/documents/ASV_Pr ogram_Guide_v3.1.pdf?agreement=true&time=1560852 761444

This document provides guidance and requirements applicable to ASVs in the framework of the PCI DSS and associated payment brand data protection programmes. Security scanning companies interested in providing scan services as part of the PCI programme must comply with the requirements set out in this document, and must complete the PCI SSC Security Scanning Vendor Testing and Approval Process.

CHAPTER 12: THE PCI DSS AND ISO/IEC 27001

ISO/IEC 27001 is the international information security management standard that more and more organisations are using to ensure that their information security management meets the data protection and compliance requirements of a wide variety of legislation, including the EU's General Data Protection Regulation (GDPR) and the Directive on security of network and information systems (NIS2 Directive), the US's HIPAA and GLBA, and others.

While the PCI DSS was not written to map specifically to ISO 27001 or to any other existing framework, it sits clearly within the ISO 27001 framework, and organisations that have implemented an ISO 27001 information security management system (ISMS) should be able, with minor additional work, to also demonstrate their conformance with the PCI DSS. The individual controls detailed in the PCI DSS can be mapped to the controls and clauses of ISO 27001 (primarily to Annex A, the list of information security controls).

It certainly makes sense for any organisation that is pursuing either ISO 27001 or PCI DSS compliance, and has both payment card data and other confidential data (whether personally identifiable information – sometimes known as 'PII' – or other commercial information) to protect, to tackle the requirements of the PCI DSS from within the ISO 27001 framework.

CHAPTER 13: THE SOFTWARE SECURITY FRAMEWORK (SSF)

The Software Security Framework (SSF) is the PCI SSC-managed programme that focuses on payment applications, such as shopping carts, payment gateways, and so on. It comprises the Secure Software Standard (SSS) and the Secure SLC (software lifecycle) Standard. These replace the old PA-DSS standard for software. Increasingly, criminals are targeting vulnerabilities in payment applications to steal payment card data, and some users may unknowingly have sensitive card data stored on their systems by software. The SSF is therefore meant to help software vendors and others develop secure payment applications that do not store prohibited data, such as full magnetic stripes, CVV2 or personal identification number (PIN) data, and to ensure their payment applications support compliance with the PCI DSS.

The SSS applies to commercial off-the-shelf (COTS) payment software that is sold, distributed or licensed to third parties. This includes payment software intended to be installed on customer systems and Software as a Service (SaaS) delivered in the Cloud. In-house or bespoke payment applications that are developed by merchants or service providers and not sold to a third party are not subject to the SSS requirements, but must still comply with the PCI DSS.

The Secure SLC Standard may apply to entities that develop COTS payment software and to entities that develop bespoke and custom software for their own use or for a single customer.

Use of SSS-certified software or software developed by an SLC-certified developer may enable an entity to consider certain sub-requirements within requirement six as in place.

The SSS and Secure SLC Standard have their own security audit procedures and their own detailed programme guides[9] that help organisations determine exactly how these compliance requirements affect them. The PCI SSC also publishes and maintains a list of Validated Payment Software[10] and Secure SLC Qualified Software Vendors that have been assessed as having met the requirements of the Standard. As these lists are continually updated, we recommend that merchants contact the respective software vendors to confirm that their applications are fully compliant with the latest version of the SSF.

As mentioned in Chapter 6, we strongly recommend using a third-party payment gateway service that is fully PCI compliant, particularly for the requirements of a small e-commerce business. While such a service provider is not obliged to use an in-house software application that is compliant with the SSF, we advise that merchants use the larger suppliers that are fully compliant with the SSF and the PCI DSS.

---

[9] *https://docs-prv.pcisecuritystandards.org/Software%20Security/Supporting%20Document/PCI-Secure-Software-Program-Guide-v1_2.pdf.* *https://docs-prv.pcisecuritystandards.org/Software%20Security/Supporting%20Document/PCI-Secure-SLC-Program-Guide-v1_1.pdf.*
[10] *https://www.pcisecuritystandards.org/assessors_and_solutions/software_lifecycle.*

CHAPTER 14: PIN TRANSACTION SECURITY (PTS)

The PCI SSC also has compliance requirements for PIN-entry (PIN pad and POS) devices that are used in conjunction with payment cards in environments attended by a cashier, merchant or sales clerk, or those that are unattended, such as garage forecourts. (These are also frequently known as PEDs or PDQs.) There is a testing and approval guide,[11] together with detailed vendor guidance on how to gain approval.

The PIN Security Requirements document contains a complete set of requirements for the secure management, processing and transmission of PIN data during online and offline payment card transaction processing at ATMs, and attended and unattended POS terminals.

The PIN Transaction Security programme includes unattended payment terminals (UPTs) and hardware security modules (HSMs), so that these devices can be rigorously tested to ensure they secure cardholder data in a payment process. UPTs include self-service ticketing machines, kiosks, automated fuel pumps and vending machines. HSMs are secure cryptographic devices that can be used for PIN translation, card personalisation, electronic commerce or data protection, and do not include any type

---

[11] *https://docs-prv.pcisecuritystandards.org/PTS/Supporting%20Document/PTS_Program_Guide_v2.1a.pdf*.

of cardholder interface. The PCI SSC maintains a list of approved UPTs and HSMs.

www.pcisecuritystandards.org/assessors_and_solutions/pi n_transaction_devices.

Merchants using point-of-interaction devices should ensure that they are PTS certified.

CHAPTER 15: POINT-TO-POINT ENCRYPTION (P2PE)

The P2PE programme covers payment products that ensure the encryption of account data at the point of first entry (i.e. at a point-of-interaction device) through to its subsequent processing at a payment service provider.[12] Certification may apply to an entire end-to-end solution offered by a P2PE solution provider or to the individual components that make up a solution: P2PE applications, PTS devices, decryption services and key-management services. Individual validated components may be combined to form a bespoke solution.

Use of a validated P2PE solution may simplify PCI DSS compliance for a merchant that will likely qualify to use SAQ P2PE for that payment channel.

The PCI SSC lists P2PE solutions that have been validated by a P2PE assessor.

https://www.pcisecuritystandards.org/assessors_and_solutions/point_to_point_encryption_solutions

---

[12] *https://docs-prv.pcisecuritystandards.org/P2PE/Supporting%20Document/PCI-SSC_P2PE_Program_Guide_v3.0r1.0.pdf.*

CHAPTER 16: SOFTWARE-BASED PIN ENTRY ON COMMERCIAL OFF-THE-SHELF (COTS) DEVICES

The PCI SSC publishes a standard for software-based PIN entry on COTS devices, such as smartphones and tablets. The PCI Software-Based PIN Entry (SPoC) Standard provides a software-based approach for protecting PIN entry on the wide variety of COTS devices on the market today. The security requirements are for solution providers to use in developing secure solutions that enable EMV contact and contactless transactions with PIN entry on the merchant's consumer device using a secure PIN-entry application in combination with a Secure Card Reader for PIN (SCRP).

The Standard comprises two documents – Security Requirements and Test Requirements:

- Security Requirements are objectives for the solution provider that designs the overall solution or components, such as the application that receives the PIN. The Security Requirements can also help other organisations understand expectations for securing these types of payments.
- The Test Requirements create validation mechanisms for payment security laboratories to evaluate the security of a solution. A supporting programme lists PCI-validated software-based PIN-entry solutions on the PCI SSC website for merchant use.

Use of a validated P2PE solution may simplify PCI DSS compliance for a merchant that will likely qualify to use SAQ SPoC for that payment channel.

FURTHER READING

IT Governance Publishing (ITGP) is the world's leading publisher for governance and compliance. Our industry-leading pocket guides, books and training resources are written by real-world practitioners and thought leaders. They are used globally by audiences of all levels, from students to C-suite executives.

Our high-quality publications cover all IT governance, risk and compliance frameworks and are available in a range of formats. This ensures our customers can access the information they need in the way they need it.

Our other resources about PCI DSS include:

- *IT Governance – An international guide to data security and ISO 27001/ISO 27002, Eighth edition* by Alan Calder and Steve Watkins, *www.itgovernance.co.uk/shop/product/it-governance-an-international-guide-to-data-security-and-iso-27001iso-27002-eighth-edition*
- CyberComply, *www.itgovernance.co.uk/shop/product/cybercomply*
- PCI DSS Foundation Self-Paced Online Training Course, *www.itgovernance.co.uk/shop/product/pci-dss-foundation-self-paced-online-training-course*

For more information on ITGP and branded publishing services, and to view our full list of publications, please visit

www.itgovernancepublishing.co.uk.

To receive regular updates from ITGP, including information on new publications in your area(s) of interest, sign up for our newsletter at *www.itgovernancepublishing.co.uk/topic/newsletter*.

Branded publishing

Through our branded publishing service, you can customise ITGP publications with your organisation's branding. Find out more at

www.itgovernancepublishing.co.uk/topic/branded-publishing-services.

Related services

ITGP is part of GRC International Group, which offers a comprehensive range of complementary products and services to help organisations meet their objectives.

For a full range of PCI DSS resources, please visit *www.itgovernance.co.uk/pci_dss*.

Training services

The IT Governance training programme is built on our extensive practical experience designing and implementing management systems based on ISO standards, best practice and regulations.

Our courses help attendees develop practical skills and comply with contractual and regulatory requirements. They also support career development via recognised qualifications.

Learn more about our training courses and view the full course catalogue at

www.itgovernance.co.uk/training.

Professional services and consultancy

We are a leading global consultancy of IT governance, risk management and compliance solutions. We advise organisations around the world on their most critical issues and present cost-saving and risk-reducing solutions based on international best practice and frameworks.

We offer a wide range of delivery methods to suit all budgets, timescales and preferred project approaches.

Find out how our consultancy services can help your organisation at

www.itgovernance.co.uk/consulting.

Industry news

Want to stay up to date with the latest developments and resources in the IT governance and compliance market? Subscribe to our Security Spotlight newsletter and we will send you mobile-friendly emails with fresh news and features about your preferred areas of interest, as well as unmissable offers and free resources to help you successfully start your project: *www.itgovernance.co.uk/security-spotlight-newsletter*.

.

EU for product safety is Stephen Evans, The Mill Enterprise Hub, Stagreenan, Drogheda, Co. Louth, A92 CD3D, Ireland. (servicecentre@itgovernance.eu)

www.ingramcontent.com/pod-product-compliance
Lightning Source LLC
Chambersburg PA
CBHW042315210326
41599CB00038B/7140